Military Cadence Candy 3

"Calloholic"

Author

Brett E. Thomas

Contributors

Kareena A. Thomas

Jenna K. Thomas

John C. Turner

Joe Whitner

ISBN-13: 978-1726274838
ISBN-10: 1726274837

DEDICATION

Military Cadence Candy 3 is dedicated to military members that search for the good in everything. We wrote these cadences to motivate, uplift and inspire all who choose to read, memorize and call them.

INTRODUCTION

Just like Military Cadence Candy 1 and 2, Military Cadence Candy 3 has been tried and truly enjoyed by our Military all around the world. This book stands out to the masses because the cadences are uplifting and positive affirmations. One line of cadence is sung by the cadence caller. Unless noted otherwise-that exact line is repeated by the formation. Motivational cadences bring out the best in everyone. Feel free to edit any questionable words or phrases to keep them politically correct. Imagination and rhythm play a major key in cadence calling. Military Cadence Candy is separated into two parts-Marching Cadence Candy and Running Cadence Candy. Every verse is counted as one line of cadence unless noted otherwise.

All Military branches will enjoy perusing this vast collection of original cadences...Military Cadence Candy 3 "Calloholic".

MARCHING CADENCE CANDY

RUNNING CADENCE CANDY

MARCHING CADENCE CANDY

A MATTER OF TIME – MARCHING

It's just a matter of time

Before you see success

Focus on your goals

Perseverance is the key

The key to success

It's just a matter of time

Pockets get fatter with dimes

Save, some of what you earn

Live, and learn

It's just a matter of time

It takes twenty-one years

To be twenty-one

There are no short cuts

The elevator is broke

You must take the stairs

Step up to the plate

It's just a matter of time

ADRENALIN RUSH - MARCHING

I get an adrenalin rush

From feeling your touch

Like a cinnamon slush

I'm in it like a crush

It being us

We go together

Like cloths and tailors

Like wool and leather

Our love is good

And it could be better

I pray we last

Through the bad weather

If we don't rush

We can last forever

Just like sand

In the Sahara

I'm the man

That's in your mirror

See me when

Your (pin) is cleaned up (firing pin)

I never felt this way before

Got me open like a sea shore

All gassed up like Ford Explorer

Weapon, I adore ya

I'll do anything for ya

I get an adrenalin rush

ALL AROUND THE WORLD - MARCHING

All around the world and back again

All the way up the mountain and through the hill

All around the world and back again

Up the boulevard and around the loop

All around the world and back again

Through the street and down the road

All around the world and back again

On the avenue down the way

All around the world and back again

AUTHENTIC AUTHOR - MARCHING

Cadence caller, authentic author

Face the music and salute me partner

Like I got fifty stars and thirteen stripes

I represent blood, sweat and life

Hardcore with the motivation

Fired up with the dedication

BAD MAN -MARCHING

I'm a bad man

I'm a baaaad maaaan

The way I drum up cadence

I leave (snares) torn (snare drum)

Bald eagle on the beat

Like my hair gone

Take flight on the mic

Like I'm Airborne

I've stepped my game up

I left the stairs worn

Now I see why

They scared of my storm

I got my eyes on the prize

Like I'm staring at a throne

Godly with the Cadence Candy

I leave the devil scorned

Okay you've been warned

I blossom on the trail

Like a rose with thorns

Kill the B.S. (bull$h!t)

And walk away with the horns

I'm a bad man

I'm a baaaaad maaaan

BASKETBALL - MARCHING

Saturday morning about a quarter to ten

I go to the gym and get it in

I ask "who got next?"

I ask "you got five?"

I ask "can I play?"

We go live

I get in the post notify the dispatch

I'm a truck on the court, mismatch

I'm on fire like a lit match

Torching competition

All revved up

Like a key in the ignition

Saturday morning about a quarter to ten

Who's hooping?

You hooping?

I'm hooping!

Come see me!

BEAT BOX- MARCHING

Cadence Caller: (Beat Box) Booba doom sck doom oom oom sck oom

Column 1of formation: (Beat Box)

Cadence Caller: "Okay column 1 be quiet, column 2 say On and on and on."

Column 2: On and on and on.

Cadence Caller: "Okay column 2 be quiet, column 3 say Keep going, keep going."

Column 3: Keep going, keep going.

Cadence Caller: "Okay column 3 be quiet, column 4 say We here now."

Column 4: We here now!

Cadence Caller: "Okay, everybody together!

Column 1: (Beat Box)

Column 2: "On and on and on!"

Column 3: "Keep going, keep going!"

Column 4: "We here now!"

C1C2C3C4

O O O O < Formation

O O O O

Cadence Caller > O   O O O O

O O O O

O O O O

Notes: Cadence Caller keeps formation in rhythm by beat boxing. (Beat boxing is making music with your mouth)

Cadence Caller can also have formation as a whole repeat each line together.

Example:

Cadence Caller: (Beat Box)

Formation: (Beat Box)

CC: On and on and on!

F: On and on and on!

CC: Keep going, keep going!

F: Keep going, keep going!

BE PREPARED- MARCHING

Be prepared and ready always ready

I'm stating facts

I'm not lying

I'm a cool cat

Look at me and see a lion

Self-esteem through the roof

Confidence is my cologne

I reek boss player

With the power of reason

I heat all haters

Tough skin like a gator

I'll serve you like a waiter

Do yourself a favor

Be prepared and ready

BOOTS AND CATS (BEAT BOX)- MARCHING

Boots and cats and boots and cats

Dooga dooga dooga dooga dooga

Gagoom gagoom gagoom brrrrrit

Keep going, keep keep going

Oomp ta uh ta oomp oomp uh

Boots and cats and boots and cats

Oomp ta uh ta oomp oomp uh

Keep going, keep keep going

Gagoom gagoom gagoom brrrrrit

Dooga dooga dooga dooga dooga

Note: Picture the words as sound effects. (Beatbox) each word or exchange the words for sound effects, screams, noise etc. (Beat boxing is making music with your mouth)

BOOTS TO BUSINESS- MARCHING

Boots to business

Entrepreneurship

Track of the transition

Transition assistance

A three-part program

First an info video

Then a two-day course

With subject matter experts

Next the third part

Is an eight-week course

Log in online

And create a business plan

Think, different

Jump in with both feet

Be all in

Get smart as you go

You just have to go

Take massive action

Towards your goal

Create and innovate

Pursue happiness

Entrepreneurship

Your key to freedom

Boot to business

CONFIDENCE- MARCHING

With confidence

You will find away

A way to win

With confidence

You will find a way

To make it through (ooh ooh oo) Stretch-out the word through

Confidence

CRAZY TRUTH- MARCHING

I stepped in the game speaking crazy truth

Father of the top like I raised the roof

Cheddar (money) so heavy you can't gauge my loot

Every cadence fire, nearly blazed my tooth

Volcano with the flow, call me lava lips

I been this way since audio cassette

Moving through the top with pep in my step

I will never stop with the rep of a vet

I stepped in the game speaking crazy truth

DESTINY- MARCHING

The roads we take

Are more important than

The goals we announce

Decisions determine

Des-ti-ny

Take action

Talk less

Make sound decisions Decide your path

The roads we take

Become our destiny

Decisions determine

Destiny (Des-ti-ny)

DISTRACTED DRIVING- MARCHING

Distracted driving

That's a no go

Don't text and drive

Arrive alive

Drive sixty-five (miles per hour)

Just follow signs

Stay in the lines

High alert

Check your tires first

Don't die of thirst

No need to speed

Drive safely

Distracted driving

That's a no go

Don't text and drive

You see someone doing it

Blow your horn

Gesture for them to stop (Hanging up the phone gesture)

And keep it going

Distracted driving

That's a no go

DO ANYTHING- MARCHING

What would you do

If you could do anything

Would you rent a plane?

Ride in it with your main

Squeeze please believe

(Big Serge) Will achieve

With C's and B's

Perhaps an A+ (plus)

I'll never get enough of this

From dawn to dusk

What would you do

EVERYONE (BY KEN KEYES, JR) – MARCHING

Everyone

And everything

Around you

Is your teacher

Everyone and everything

Around you, is your teacher

FOCUS- MARCHING

Focus on the task at hand

Lock in on your goals

Make informed decisions

Fulfill your obligations

Work for a bigger cause

Other than yourself

Do what's right

Have no fear

Focus on the task at hand

FOOLISH- MARCHING

Fool me once

Shame on you

Fool me twice

Shame on me

I'll act a fool

To fool a fool

Reel him in

Like a fishing spool

Call him fish and chips

Or chicken chew

I have a mission

I'm sticking to

Fool me once

Shame on you

GO TO GUY- MARCHING

Go to guy, go, go to guy

Go to guy, go, go to guy

Make impossible possible

Conquer colossal obstacles

Any city we're marching through

Turn the city to romper rooms

Boots on stomping you

Like some ghost we're haunting you

Even if you don't want us to

Go to guy, go, go to guy

I CREPT- MARCHING

I crept out of nowhere

Right at his post

He looked at me wide eyed

Like he saw a ghost

Because I had the "clip" in (magazine)

And he saw my "toast" (weapon)

I cocked back and sent shots

Through the seam of his cloths

He hit the ground

I put the beam on his nose

It was rude and bazar

Like those dudes at the bazaar

He tried to play tough

He was acting by far

No time for lollygagging

Or squealing like a sorry wagon

I crept up out of nowhere

I KNOW- MARCHING

I know a man with a plan

That man with the plan is me

I know a woman with an idea

That woman took action on her idea

I know a Soldier with a dream

That Soldier took action on his dream

I know a Marine that's motivated

A devil dog who's true

I know a Sailor who succeeded

Success for Sailor is swell

I know an Airmen with a great attitude

That great attitude helps him excel

I NEED YOU (BY JENNA THOMAS)-
MARCHING

I need you to know

That I know, you're not perfect

But in my eyes

You're still a superhero

You wear a crown not a halo

And trust, I need you to know

That I know the difference

I need you to try everyday

Stop being scared of you

I need you to use your fear

Your life can be easy to blame

I need you to hold on tight

But still let yourself go

I need you to know

IF YOU SEE ME- MARCHING

If you see me in the dark

Or the light of the day

You're looking at my back

As I'm walking away

You'll see the back of my head

As I'm breaking my bread

Standing on my own two

As an example, to my kids

If you see me in the dark

Or the light of thc day

LEFT, RIGHT, LEFT (SOLDIER) – MARCHING

Left, right, left (Soldier)

Saddle up (Soldier)

Drive on (Soldier)

Buck up (Soldier)

Keep going (Soldier)

All night long (Soldier)

Rock steady (Soldier)

Roll ready (Soldier)

Note: (soldier) can be changed to Marine, Airmen, Sailor, Reservist or Guardsmen

MAIL CALL- MARCHING

Mail call

Mail call

It's music to my ears

You must write a letter

To receive a letter

P. O. Box

Send and receive

Mail call

Mail call

It's music to my ears

Reach out

The more the better

A care package

For a letter

Mail call

Mail call

It's music to my ears

MISS ME- MARCHING

Miss me with that tough talk

I'm standing on a chess board

I'm on top of my game

If you're only playing checkers

We're not talking the same

Cool and calm when I speak

Barking is lame

Drive by you with the big guns

Then park it to aim

My words leave welts

Like an unruly dad

I'll school you by the numbers

You do the math

Miss me with that tough talk

MY IDEAS- MARCHING

These are my ideas

Explained in plain English

Don't point fingers

Don't blame strangers

Aim your banger (weapon)

Then change the angle

Then float like angels

Main I'm dangerous

Goody two boots

Get circled like fruit loops

I'm raising my brand

And you can't get two scoops

These are my ideas

MY OWN EYES- MARCHING

Clear blue skies

Star filled nights

I see it with my own eyes

Rainy days and snow storms

I see it with my own eyes

What, I'm saying is

I saw the worst

I saw bubbles float

I saw bubbles burst

Saw the enemies in cuffs

Saw them in a Hurst

I saw a healthy man

Dying of thirst

I can see the light

With the greatest of ease

I can see the big picture

And get you to believe

Anything is possible

Just gather your steps

And hop over obstacles

Clear blue skies

I saw it with my own eyes

ONE HUNDO- MARCHING

If you give me ninety-nine percent

You are dead wrong

Like texting at a green light

You know that's not right

I need one hundred

Good old' one hundo

One hundred percent from you

One hundred percent from me

Go all out all day

Go all out all night

Give me one hundred percent

Good old' one hundo

OPPORTUNITIES- MARCHING

Opportunities knock, I "swing the hinges" (open the door)

Allow me to engulf your senses

With these sharp utensils

Feeding you "lead", no parts of the pencil (bullets)

You don't need the eraser

You need to embrace it

Or my feet where your face is

I'll give you a face lift

Get the ugly look off your face

Like braces

PERFECT TIME- MARCHING

It's a perfect time

To search your mind

It's a perfect time

To seek and find

It's a perfect time

To upgrade your life

It's a perfect time

To deal with strife

It's a perfect time

To appreciate

It's a perfect time

To not hate

It's a perfect time

PRACTICE WHAT YOU PREACH- MARCHING

Practice what you preach

Do what you say

Walk the talk

Be true to your word

Keep your promises

Practice what you preach

I would do

What I tell you to do

I have done

What I told you to do

Practice what you preach

QUICK TO LISTEN- MARCHING

Be quick to listen

Slow to anger

Don't come at me sideways

I know the angle

Keep enemies close

Foes get strangled

(Super Trooper)

Down to my ankles

RUMOR HAS IT- MARCHING

Rumor has it

You use gadgets

Send you to a tomb

With the maggots

Tragedy magnet

Note: This short and sweet cadence is for transitioning to another cadence. It can be used over and over.

SEE ME- MARCHING

See me in the battle

Ruck sack like a camel

More ammo then Rambo

Unseen in my camo

Jumping like hopscotch

Topnotch with these "hot rocks" (bullets)

Dedicated 'til my heart stops

See me in the battle

Hot to the touch like a candle

Nobody does it better

Withstanding any weather

Rain, sleet or snow

Etcetera, etcetera

 I monster up often

More power than Osten (Osten Powers)

So, what will it be? You battle me?

You battle me then suffer defeat

Get in where you fit, mission complete

See me in the battle

SHINE- MARCHING

Shine like a lighthouse

See through the dark

Just like a night owl

Take it to the upper level

Forget being a failure

Shine like a lighthouse

Let me see your sun shine through

Let me see your clear blue sky

Let me see your rainbow baby

Let your true colors shine

Shine like a light house

SHOW ME (BY JENNA THOMAS) -MARCHING

I will show you I can shine

I will show you the beauty

But first you have to show me

Show me what it means to protect

Show me how to follow the rules

Show me how to cross the lines

Show me the strength of consistency

Show me power in focused energy

Show me how I'm supposed to be treated

Show how to command respect

Show me what high standards are

Show me what it looks like to love

If you show me I will surprise you!

I will show you I can shine

SOME SAY I'M WRONG- MARCHING

Some say I'm wrong for how I act

I act like a (Soldier)

What's wrong with that

I lay enemies on their back

I blow 'em up then stay intact

I'm fighting for freedom

You know that's a fact

I've been to Iraq

But now I'm back

Check my combat patch

I lift the lock off the latch

Light, you up 'til you fade to black

Some say I'm wrong for how I act

STEALING- MARCHING

Note: Call this cadence differently each time a verse is repeated. "Jazz it up" each time around.

The *(Man) that buys

What he does not need

Steals from *(himself)

Buy what you need

Don't steal from yourself

Don't steal period

*Woman / herself

*Troop / himself/herself

*Sailor/ himself/herself

*Seamen/ himself/herself

*Marine/ himself/herself

*Soldier/ himself/herself

*Civilian/ himself/herself

STEEL SHARPENS STEEL- MARCHING

Steel sharpens steel

Iron sharpens iron

We got your back

Like a pride of lions

Steel sharpens steel

Iron sharpens iron

Hard to the core

And a live wire

Steel sharpens steel

SUPER TROOPER- MARCHING

Super trooper with a vengeance

Horrendously stupendous

Check the census I'm an instant

Super troop extraordinaire

So prepared, so much flair

No seat back I'm sitting there

I'm everywhere like smoke in the air

Like paint out of a pail

I spread out like email

Make more success than I fail

Wish me luck as I knuckle up

Super trooper with a vengeance

THE ONES I LOVE- MARCHING

This is dedicated to the ones I love

Everything I do

I do it for you

Do it in the morning

Do it in the afternoon

Rock steady all night

I get in the groove

High key!

High key!

High key!

This is dedicated to the ones I love

THE REALEST- MARCHING

I'm the realest person I know

I'm the ultimate hunter

You can act like you're running the show

You're just the alternate runner

I shut down runways

Airplanes are not flyer

I standout like letters

Under highlighters

Aura of a sensei

Call me Meiyagi

Leave them all aw struck

Like I pulled up

In a Maserati

I'm ultra-original

 Never been a carbon copy

I'm the realest person I know

THREE- MARCHING

I will guard everything!

Within the limits of my post!

And quit my post only

When properly relieved!

I will obey my special orders

And perform all my duties

In a military manner

I will report violations

Emergencies and anything

Not covered in my instructions

To the commander of the relief

TROUBLE- MARCHING

Trouble came up to me the other day

He said "I got a plan to get you on your way"

"This plan that I have can get you hella pay"

"All you have to do is agree and say okay"

I said "Hella?" and laughed a little bit

Then turned my ear up like Old Yella

Trouble tried to play cool

Like he was a fan

So, I called him by his name

I said "Trouble, what's your plan"

He said "Aw man, check this out"

"You can sell crack and get big clout"

"Without a doubt get cash"

"Be in then be out"

I said "No thanks", and went on my way

You win some you some

But you live

You live to fight another day

WOKE- MARCHING

Woke up this morning in a good mood

Washed my hands and brushed my teeth

Swiggled with a little bit of mouthwash

Brushed my tong then flossed

Then I swiggled with a little bit of water

Then I drank a little water from my cup

I looked myself in the mirror

Turned on the water grabbed a washcloth

Wet my cloth then washed my face

Brushed my hair and went on my way

Thankful for this day

Woke up this morning in a good mood

WORK MY FINGERS- MARCHING

Work my fingers to the bone

Like a singer on the throne

Call you out at my show

Like (Jerry) Springer on the phone

I'm down to get that (doe/dough) (money)

Like a deer with the horns

No fear when I perform

Give you your monies worth

Like a rose without the thorns

Give you the naked truth

Like I pose without the cloths

Double up on what I do

Like I'm rolling with a clone

Work my fingers to the bone

RUNNING CADENCE CANDY

BEARDED LIZARD – RUNNING

Seen a bearded lizard sitting on a wall

Sitting at the top, above it all

He had a lizard friend with reverse scales

They both loved to wheel and deal

Command told bearded lizard, see the nurse

He saw the doctor and the news was the worst

Doctor gave bearded lizard a permanent profile

Told him not to shave for a very long while

Remember lizard friend with the reverse scales?

He shaved every morning, got the good details

The moral of the story is

You want the good details, shave your beard

And if you don't have reverse scales

Get yourself a permanent deal (Profile)

Seen a bearded lizard sitting on a wall

BRAIN WASHED – RUNNING

You know how I know you're brain washed?

You still sidestep in the chow line

You know how I know you're brain washed?

You tell the barber "high and tight"

You know how I know you're brain washed?

Your mom says "Hi" you say "Hooah"

You know how I know you're brain washed?

You wear a Kevlar in your car

You know how I know you're brain washed?

You wear running shoes with jeans

You know how I know you're brain washed?

If we out of uniform you, call me by my rank

You know how I know you're brain washed?

CALLOHOLIC – RUNNING

Cadence candy Calloholic

Don't talk mess to us

Save it for the toilet

We're winning in the end

Sorry that I spoiled it

Cadence Candy Calloholic

Bears with the cadences

You can say we maul it

We'll pull up at the mall quick

Brawl until we fall "Bae" (Baby□)

Ayeee, we're all in

Cadence Candy Calloholic

CHECK – RUNNING

Check my war wounds, check

I'm a war vet, check

Wheels to the road, check

Like a corvette, check

Vroom, vroom, vroom, check

Wild like a baboon, check

Using enemies, check

Like a bathroom, check

I'm dodoing on them, check

So they are pissed, check

Get dismissed, check

Quick like a toothpick, check

Longarm of the law, check

Like a blue stick, check

Ill Cadence Calloholic, check

You can say my flow sick, check

CHEMIST – RUNNING

Chemist with the cadences

I concoct remedies

Tasty, cadences

Like my grandma's recipes

You don't want to mess with me

Cadence calling is my destiny

I'm a million steps a head

Call me Mr. Millipede

Quick witted

So gifted

Like an cscalator

I'll get you lifted

Don't be a player hater

Don't be tempted

To stop my shine

But keep in mind

I'm on my grind

Like bad brakes

Cadences connected

Like sausage links

CHOO CHOO TRAIN – RUNNING

Note: * = Beat Box or Sound effects

I'm a choo choo train on the track

*I'm a chook chook tre on da tra

I'm a freight train on the run

*I'm ah fre tra on da ruh

I'm a steam engine in this thing

*I'm a ste eng in dis thi

I go beast mode on the beat

*I gah beam o on da beea

CIRCUS ANTICS – RUNNING

Circus antics with the cadence

Call me Barnum and Bailey
Hold that trash talk

Let it burn in your belly

I'm on the road to riches

You're on a journey for jelly

I'm not concerned with that

I believe whatever you tell me

I'm wonderful with it

Wild as a jungle of misfits

DEPOSITS – RUNNING

Deposit just hit

About to pay some bills

Get some holy water

Just a cheap little thrill

Been working all week

Training to kill

Now I'm ready for whatever

Because I'm the real deal

Deposit just hit

DIAMOND DIGGER – RUNNING

I'm a diamond digger

I mine my business

I apply that pressure

I'm a diamond digger

I mine my skill

I mine my craft

I'm a diamond digger

I apply that pressure

Pressure burst pipes?

Pressure don't faze me

I'm digging for diamonds

I'm a diamond digger

DON'T WASTE MY TIME – RUNNING

Don't waste my time

Don't waste my time

Don't waste my time

You, never saw me slack

Yo Simity Sam when I send the mack (shot bullets)

Rootin' tootin' raasin fraasin

Everlasting you better blast when

You see me stepping in this thing

With verbal weapons, I'm the (King/Queen)

You pitching woo like Jinga Ling

Whining to your crew about everything

Don't waste my time

GET RID OF IT – RUNNING

Get rid of it

Get rid of it

Nasty attitude

Get rid of it

Contraband

Get rid of it

Hair under your chin

Get rid of it

Trash bin full?

Get rid of it

Dirty mop water

Get rid of it

That negative vibe

Get rid of it

HANDS UP – RUNNING

Put your hands up

Put your hands down

I'm feeling good

Let's run a mile

Put your hands up

Put your hands through

I'm feeling great

Let's run two

Put your hands out

Tall like a tree

I'm feeling grand

Let's run three

HAPPY BIRTHDAY...WHAT? – RUNNING

Happy birthday, it's not my birthday, what?

Live everyday

Like it's your birthday

Happy birthday, it's not my birthday, what?

Live everyday

Like you want success

In the worst way

Happy birthday, it's not my birthday, what?

Eyes on the prize

First place

HEY YOUNG – RUNNING

Hey young hero

It's real in the field

That's no metaphor

Been there done that

Now I'm better for it

Hey young hero

It's real on the tour

That's no metaphor

Been there done that

Now I'm better for it

HIGH POWERED – RUNNING

Cadence Caller: When that left foot strikes the street, all I want to hear is "I'm high powered"

Formation: I'm high powered!

CC: I'm high powered

Formation: I'm high powered!

CC: I'm winning in the end

Formation: I'm high powered!

CC: My mind is a gem

Formation: I'm high powered!

CC: I just do it

Formation: I'm high powered!

CC: Then do it again

Formation: I'm high powered!

CC: This we'll defend

Formation: I'm high powered!

CC: I'm winning in the end

HOLD IT DOWN – RUNNING

I hold it down

I hold it down

I hold it down

Like a rail pin

Freight train on the run

Force of a whirlwind

 Want to know if I rock

Ask your girlfriend

I up-chuck cadences

The way I hurl gems

I broaden minds

Ask your broad or mine

I shape futures

Check the way I "shoot it" (Give it to you)

I hold it down

HOW FAST – RUNNING

They said "how fast are you"

I said "faster than a track star"

No one hundred-meter dash

I'm talking NASCAR

Supersonic space speed

 Now I'm talking NASA

Out of this world

Teach nothing but truth

To help you seek and improve

I asked "how fast are you?"

HYPED – RUNNING

Get hyped up!

Tuned in

Turnt up

On ten!

You're level five?

That's way too quiet

Turn it up

Get hyped up

Hyped up

I DON'T SMOKE PORTS – RUNNING

I don't smoke ports (Newport cigs)

I smoke Joes

So wet behind the ears

They're wearing soaked cloths

Cadence Candy cadences

By the boat loads

Even Bo knows

I got dope flows

And without a Fort

To face foes

I stand my ground

And hold it down

Like a ratchet strap

Explode on the run

Watch you catch the scraps

Running the game

Like a batch of laps

Adding light to your life

Like a batch of matches

Crashing with mental food

Passionate interludes

I JUMP IN – RUNNING

I jump in and double-time

You're in trouble when I rhyme

I rock the mic to bed

Like Barney Rubble in his prime

I'm always in the game

I never fumble with the pine (bench)

Super straight shooter

Like a ruler on my nine (gun)

Mentor on the run

School you with every line

I jump in and double-time

I'M NEXT LEVEL – RUNNING

I'm next level always

I saw the devil in the hallway

He said "I'll be here all day"

I kicked the devil in his head

Left him with a bald fade

Then walked down some stairs

The theme song from "Jaws" played

I'm next level always

I'M SWIMMING – RUNNING

I'm swimming through this tour

Shark Attack!

You looked for me out front

But I parked in the back

Came to where you were and

Sparked your hat

And I'm not talking patrol

Yet I'm as cold as an arctic cap

I hope you see the art in that

I'm swimming through this tour

I'M THE – RUNNING

I'm not the baker

I'm the baker's son

I do the baker until the baker comes

I'm not the teacher I'm the teacher's son

I teach the lesson until the teacher comes

I'm not the doctor

I'm the doctor's son

I operate until the doctor comes

I'm not the chemist

I'm the chemist's son

I mix it up until the chemist comes

I'm not the lawyer

I'm the lawyer's son

I plead the case until the lawyer comes

KEEP IT ONE HUNDRED (100) – RUNNING

Keep it one hundred

Keep it real

Don't be fickle

Don't be fake

Tell me the whole truth

Don't hold back

We're grownups

No time for games

Keep it one hundred

Don't be a lame

Keep it one hundred

Keep it real

LEADERSHIP – RUNNING

What is leadership?

What's a leader?

Leaders serve

Leaders take charge

Leaders listen

Leaders go hard

Leaders focus

Leaders learn

Are you a leader?

Leaders lead

Leaders write

Leaders think

Leaders take flight

Leaders lead all-day

Leaders lead all night

What is leadership?

LET'S EAT – RUNNING

Let's eat a victory meal

After the battle

Well seasoned beef

With a salad on the side

And corn on the cob

Let's eat a victory meal

After the tour

How about some surf and turf?

Maybe a big pizza

Thin New York slice

How about that deep dish

That cheesy crust

Real big pepperonis

Let's eat a victory meal

After the war

Iceberg lettuce

Tomatoes tomawtoes

Potatoes potawtoes

What about asparagus?

Brussel sprouts

Some cool cucumbers

Let's eat a victory meal

LIFE – RUNNING

Life maybe hard

But it's not impossible

Life can be challenging

But it's not impossible

The word impossible

Says "I'm possible"

Like maybe hard

But it's not impossible

LOCKED IN – RUNNING

I'm locked in

I'm extra focused

Locked in

I'm locked in

Stone-faced

Everywhere

Like a phone case

What's the password?

There is no password!

I'm locked in

With the master key

I have the combination

I'll do you dastardly

I'm locked in

LOUD – RUNNING

Be loud in formation

Like a cry for HELP!

I get accolades and awards

You admire my shelf

Standing tall in formation

Head held high like an elk

You can try and stand your ground

I spit fire, you melt

I'm a mother father star

Like Orion's belt

I pull myself together

Like I'm tying my belt

Be loud in formation

MEANT IT – RUNNING

If I said it, I meant it

Unless I say I'm just kidding

If I say I'm just kidding

I still might have meant it

I don't beg or borrow

No pain or sorrow

Don't put off for tomorrow

Stone face to the bone marrow

Like wheels on a van truck

I go the distance

If I said it, I meant it

MR. CAUSE AND EFFECT – RUNNING

Mr. Cause and Effect

Busters talking sideways

Like a jaw on their neck

I'm leaving prints on the game

Like the paws of your pet

Mad man in this thing

I'm far from upset

(Serge) triple threat

Straight ripping through your vest

Like ripple in your chest

Mr. Cause and Effect

PARTY STARTER – RUNNING

I'm the party starter

I get the party started

I walk in a room

Here comes the boom!

I'm the party starter

I get the party started

We own the street

Mission complete

I'm the party starter

I get the party started

Even in the desert

I'm eating dessert

I'm the party starter

I get the party started

When I'm overseas

I over see

I'm the party starter

I get the party started

PEER PRESSURE – RUNNING

Peer pressure P-P-P-P-Peer pressure

Ha ha ha haha

Peer pressure P-P-P-P-Peer pressure

If pressure burst pipes

I'm adamantium

Unbreakable under pressure

No matter who's gassing him

Opinions are like finger prints

Everybody has them

I'm adamantium

Peer pressure P-P-P-P-Peer pressure

Note: Adamantium is virtually indestructible metal.

PLATOON DADDY – RUNNING

Hello

Hi Daddy

Platoon Daddy

Hello

Hi Daddy

Platoon Daddy

Beans and bullets

Beans and bullets

Beans and bullets

Take care of family

Take care of family

Take care of family

Organize the mission

Organize the mission

Organize the mission

Hello

Hi Daddy

Platoon Daddy

READ – RUNNING

Cadence Caller: When that left foot strikes the ground, all I want to hear is "Read"

Formation: Read

CC: Everybody

F: Read

CC: Learn and grow

F: Read

CC: Before you sign

F: Read

CC: The answers are written

F: Read

CC: Expand your mind

F: Read

CC: Life learners

F: Read

CC: In the library

F: Read

CC: In the Ed. center

F: Read

CC: On the weekend

F: Read

CC: On Monday

F: Read

CC: On Tuesday...

REIGNING – RUNNING

I came in the Corps reigning

No H2O I'm talking reigning

I'm on my king shhh

Don't hate or doubt

My mind I'm never bored out

ROCK AND ROLL – RUNNING

Rock and roll

On a rocky road

Smooth it out

Choose a route

Rock and roll

You're good as gold

Stay the course

Play your part

Rock and roll on a rocky road

Smooth it out, choose a route

Rock and roll, you're good as gold

Stay the course and play your part

SAFETY BRIEF – RUNNING

Safety brief

Buckle up

When you're riding around

Safety brief

Look both ways

When you cross the street

Safety brief

Call a cab

If you pop the top

Safety brief

Hard right

Over the easy wrong

Safety brief

Don't drink and swim

Don't cook naked

Let your people know

Your whereabouts

Safety brief

SCREAMING EAGLE – RUNNING

Screaming Eagle

Spread your wings

Show those feathers

Stand proud

Shoulders back

Head up

Screaming eagle

(SCREAM)

Screaming eagle

Lead the way

Soar high

Float steady

See the end

In the beginning

Drive through

Screaming eagle

(SCREAM)

Screaming eagle

SOUL FOOD – RUNNING

Soul food

Soul food

Stomach on tight

Bone in ribeye

Marinated in coco cola

Macaroni and cheese

Made from scratch

Red rice and sausage links

Stomach on tight

Home cooking is a special treat

Soul food Give me that soul food

That nourishment

That home cooking

Stomach on tight

STOP WAITING – RUNNING

What are you waiting for?

Are you waiting for sunny weather?

What are you waiting for?

Are you waiting on an email?

What are you waiting for?

Are you waiting for a memorandum?

What are you waiting for?

Are you waiting for a text message?

What are you waiting for?

Are you waiting for a phone call?

What are you waiting for?

Are you waiting for some snail mail?

What are you waiting for?

Are you waiting for a perfect time?

Do it now!

Do it now!

Stop waiting

Stop waiting

Do it now!

Do it NOW!

STRUT (BY JOHN TURNER) – RUNNING

Clap your hands and say alright

Clap your hands if you rock all night

Breath

Relax

Strut

Everybody

Rock your world

Breath

Relax

Strut

Strut your stuff

TAKING CHARGE – RUNNING

Taking charge

Is a skill

That is learned

Over time

Taking charge

Is like driving

It takes time

To learn to lead

Taking charge

Like playing piano (like playing the piano)

It takes practice

To learn to lead

TEN MUCH SAUCE – RUNNING

Too much sauce

Two much sauce

Three much sauce

Four much sauce

Five much sauce

Six much sauce

Seven much sauce

Eight much sauce

Nine much sauce

Ten much sauce

…

Fifty-five much sauce

…

One hundred much sauce

…

One million much sauce

…

One billion much sauce

THE GRING INCUDES FRIDAY (T.G.I.F.) – RUNNING

T.G.I.F.

The grind includes Friday

What about Saturday (Yeet!)

The grind includes Saturday

What about Sunday (Yeet!)

The grind includes Sunday

What about Monday (Yeet!)

The grind includes Monday

What about Tuesday (Yeet!)

The grind includes Tuesday

What about Wednesday (Yeet!)

The grind includes Wednesday

What about Thursday (Yeet!)

The grind includes Thursday

T.G.I.F.

The grind includes Friday

THANKS – RUNNING

I went to bat for you

This is the thanks that I get!

I approved thirty days leave

This is the thanks that I get!

Assigned you a cush detail

This is the thanks that I get!

Supported your decisions

This is the thanks that I get!

When you run you say "Thank You!"

This is the thanks that I get!

When you're on time you say "Thank You!"

Don't be ungrateful

Be, Thankful

THREE TYPES – RUNNING

Three types of people

Those who wait for things to happen

Those who wonder what happened

Those who make things happen

Three types of people

Which one are you

UNBELIEVABLE – RUNNING

Believe me

I'm unbelievable

My fitness scores

Are unbelievable

Believe me

I'm unbelievable

My weapons card

Is unbelievable

Believe me

I'm unbelievable

My awards rack

Is unbelievable

Believe me

I'm unbelievable

UNDENIABLE – RUNNING

Undeniable, untryable

But you can try me though

Ha, I'm just kidding bro

It doesn't hurt to try though

But' don't try me folk

I got heavenly flow

Sacred, like a Pope

Undeniable, untryable

UP IN THE MORNING (BY JOE WHITNER) – RUNNING

Up in the morning

Up in the morning

Up in the morning

Up in the morning at a quarter to three

Jumpmaster said "Come jump with me"

Open the door he had to kick me out

The whole way down I begin to shout

I said "Jesus!"

Help me!

Hold me!

Catch me!

Fired up!

Dedicated

Motivated

Ooh yeah!

All the way

Up in the morning

WATER (BY KAREENA THOMAS) – RUNNING

Water water, drink some water

If you fall down drink some water

Waters good for you and me

Drink water before PT (Physical Training)

Drink water during PT

Drink water after PT

If you're thirsty drink water

Water does the body good

Drink water with a little bit of lemon

Drink water with a little bit of lime

Drink water all the time

Canteens up

Drink until it's gone

Camel pack full of water

Drink it down

Water water drink some water

WHEN YOU TALK – RUNNING

When you talk to me

Mind your manners

I'm psycho with the cadences

My lines bananas

My flow is sewn together

Like a seamstress

My transitions (are) seamless

And you still haven't seen shhh

I make big moves

Like a team lift

When you talk to me

YOU, BATTLE ME? – RUNNING

You battle me and win?

You're sadly mistaken

I'm a boss hog

Bringing home the bacon (money)

Don't be a sugar daddy

Doing all the caking

I thought you had a clue

But you don't have an inkling

Rolling, rolling, rolling

Floating to my destination

You battle me and win?

YOU DON'T WALK – RUNNING

You don't work you don't eat

Don't ask "where the food went?"

Now I'm a "fool?"

Later follow in my footprints

You, wish I would flinch

Make moves like a mobile home

Make moves like a mobile phone

Running on your pansy pants

Forget about a landing stance

YOU MUST THINK – RUNNING

You must think it's really easy

To be this cool

Hang around with me and

Learn a lesson for sure

You cannot avoid pain

But misery is a choice

So be as quiet as you can

And hear your inner voice

You must think it's really easy

To be this cool

ZONK – RUNNING

Cadence Caller When that left foot strikes the street, all I want to hear is "Zonk"

Formation: Zonk

CC: Where you going

F: Zonk

CC: Let's hit the gym

F: Zonk

CC: Let's hit the sheets

F: Zonk

CC: Finish that homework

F: Zonk

CC: Let's get some eats

F: Zonk

CC: I'm out of here

F: Zonk

CC: Deuces

F: Zonk

CC: Thank goodness

F: Zonk

CC: Back to bed

F: Zonk

CC: Going to rest my head

F: Zonk

CC: Where you going?

AUTHOR BIOGRAPHIES

This index gives you information about each contributor and tells you where their contact information can be found.

Brett Thomas was raised in Hardeeville, South Carolina, served 13 years on active duty as a Cable Systems Installer Maintainer. Thomas is the owner and operator of *See Beyond Yourself Productions LLC DBA Surefire Youth* ™.

CONTRIBUTORS

Kareena Thomas is co-founder of *See Beyond Yourself Productions LLC DBA Surefire Youth*™. Kareena has had an illustrious career as a Child Care professional and world-renowned chief.

Jenna Thomas is a native of Hardeeville, South Carolina. She spends her time professionally as a Nurse and personally as a Mother to four Divas and loves to her feet planted in pretty sand, clear waters and sunshine.

Joe Whitner, is currently an active duty Signal Soldier. In his spare time, he enjoys creating anime, riding motorcycles, and spending time with his wife and friends. Joe is also a gifted basketball player known for his great handles and great range.

John Turner originally from Wichita Kansas is the Pastor and founder of the Community Baptist Church and Outreach Center in Sierra Vista, Arizona. He created two restaurants (Down Home Bar-B-Que and Sweet Burgers). Pastor Tuner is a veteran of the United States Marines and retired United States Army Drill Sergeant. He has added cadences to help service members ROCK STEADY!

Made in United States
Orlando, FL
17 May 2022

17969707R00067